3/04

The 3-D Library of the Human Body

THE UPPER LIMBS

LEARNING HOW WE USE OUR ARMS, ELBOWS, FOREARMS, AND HANDS

Josepha Sherman

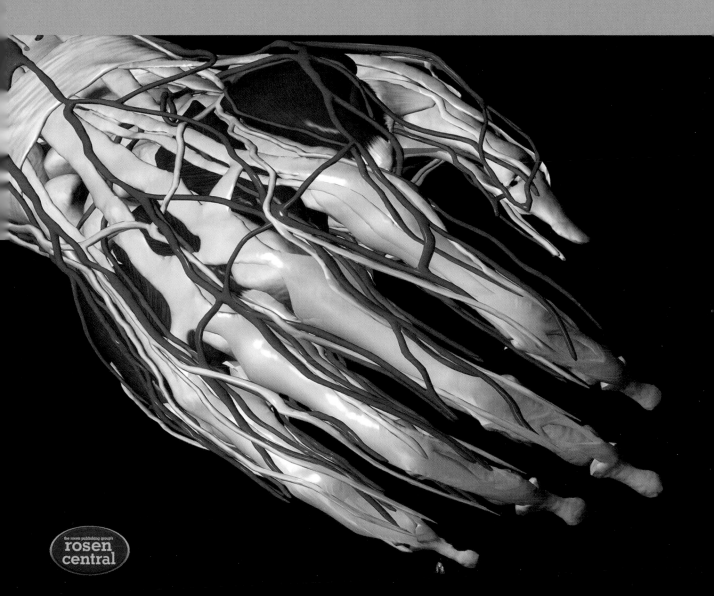

the rosen publishing group's
rosen
central

Editor's Note

The idea for the illustrations in this book originated in 1986 with the Vesalius Project at Colorado State University's Department of Anatomy and Neurobiology. There, a team of scientists and illustrators dreamed of turning conventional two-dimensional anatomical illustrations into three-dimensional computer images that could be rotated and viewed from any angle, for the benefit of students of medicine and biology. In 1988 this dream became the Visible Human Project™, under the sponsorship of the National Library of Medicine in Bethesda, Maryland. A grant was awarded to the University of Colorado School of Medicine, and in 1993 the first work of dissection and scanning began on the body of a Texas convict who had been executed by lethal injection. The process was repeated on the body of a Maryland woman who had died of a heart attack. Applying the latest techniques of computer graphics, the scientific team was able to create a series of three-dimensional digital images of the human body so beautiful and startlingly accurate that they seem more in the realm of art than science. On the computer screen, muscles, bones, and organs of the body can be turned and viewed from any angle, and layers of tissue can be electronically peeled away to reveal what lies underneath. In reproducing these digital images in two-dimensional print form, the editors at Rosen have tried to preserve the three-dimensional character of the work by showing organs of the body from different perspectives and using illustrations that progressively reveal deeper layers of anatomical structure.

Published in 2002 by The Rosen Publishing Group, Inc.
29 East 21st Street, New York, NY 10010

Digital anatomy images published by arrangement with Anatographica, LLC.
216 East 49th Street, New York, NY 10017

First Edition

Library of Congress Cataloging-in-Publication Data

Sherman, Josepha.
The upper limbs: learning how we use our arms, elbows, forearms, and hands / by Josepha Sherman. — 1st ed.
p. cm. — (The 3-D library of the human body)
Includes bibliographical references and index.
ISBN 0-8239-3537-X
1. Arm—Anatomy—Juvenile literature. 2. Shoulder—Anatomy—Juvenile literature. [1. Arm. 2. Shoulder. 3. Human anatomy.]
I. Title. II. Series.
QM548 .S46 2002
611'.97—dc21
                                                                      2001002348

Manufactured in the United States of America

CONTENTS

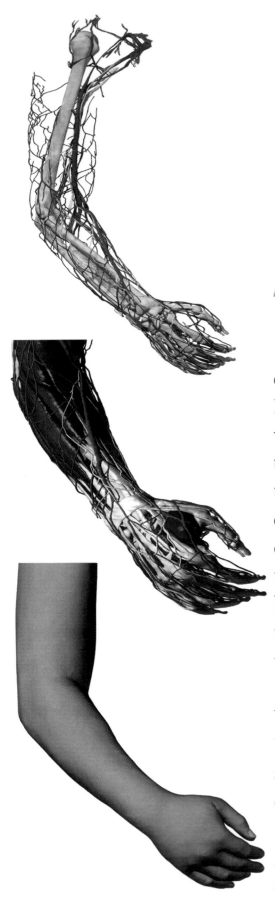

PREFACE
ART AND ANATOMY

The close historical relationship between art, science, and human anatomy is best illustrated by the career of the great Renaissance artist Leonardo da Vinci (1452–1519). Leonardo was a man of enormous curiosity about all things, and he had keen powers of observation. He also believed in the principles of science and in the idea that things should be carefully studied and observed to determine their nature. Others of his generation still believed that it was sufficient to read what the ancient Greek authorities had written to understand the world.

Leonardo was born in the Italian town of Vinci. At the age of seventeen, he moved to Florence with his father, where he was apprenticed to the artist Verrocchio. His talent as a painter was soon recognized, and in 1472 he was invited to join the painters' guild of Florence, where he met other great artists, like Michelangelo. He spent a number of years shuttling back and forth between Florence and Milan, producing great works of art and engineering for the local rulers of both cities. In 1513 he moved to Rome, where he met the painter Raphael, and in 1516 he moved to Amboise, France, where he received the patronage of the French king. He died in Amboise three years later.

Among the many subjects that interested Leonardo was the anatomy of the human body. It was natural for a painter to want to understand the structure of muscles and the other organs that gave the body its outer shape. Learned men of the time thought that the final authority on this subject was the ancient Greek physician Galen. But Galen had studied the bodies of pigs and monkeys and had simply stated that human anatomy must be similar. Leonardo went to the trouble of obtaining real human cadavers from a local morgue, and not always legally. From his dissection and study of real human bodies, Leonardo produced hundreds of precisely rendered anatomical drawings of bones and muscles and organs. He pioneered the now accepted convention of drawing organs from different perspectives so that their actual three-dimensional shapes could be understood. He was also one of the first to simplify his drawings so that individual systems—the bones, the blood vessels, the nerves—could be studied in isolation. On the pages of his drawings, he wrote many notes on the peculiarities of human organs and how to illustrate them, but he wrote them in reverse script, and to be read they must be held up to a mirror.

Leonardo's interest in anatomy stemmed not only from the fact that he was an artist but also from the fact that he was a "Renaissance man" and he believed the human body to be the "measure of all things." He called the body the "terrestrial machine," an indication of his scientific approach. His work ushered in a new era of scientific illustration based on the accurate rendering of anatomical structures.

1
THE SHOULDER AND UPPER ARM

The shoulder is one of the most flexible human joints, a ball and socket that allows the arm to move up, down, backward and forward, and even to make a complete 360-degree circle up, down, and around again. But that very flexibility makes it one of the least stable parts of the skeleton. In fact, it's hardly attached to the rest of the skeleton.

The shoulder is made up of three bones working together in the shoulder girdle. The clavicle, a slender, curved bone, is the only one that actually connects to the rest of the skeleton. Its name comes from the Latin for "key," since the bone looks like one. Most scientific names are in Latin because that was once the official language of scholars and a language that every scientist knew.

The second shoulder bone is the scapula, the wide, flatter bone at the back of the shoulder. It's also known as the shoulder blade because it does look a little like a blade. The Latin word *scapulae* means "blade." The scapula is held in place by the end of the clavicle that isn't connected to the thorax.

The third shoulder bone is the humerus, the long bone of the upper arm. Its Latin name means "upper arm." The scapula ends in a semicircular curve that leaves just enough room for the rounded top of the humerus.

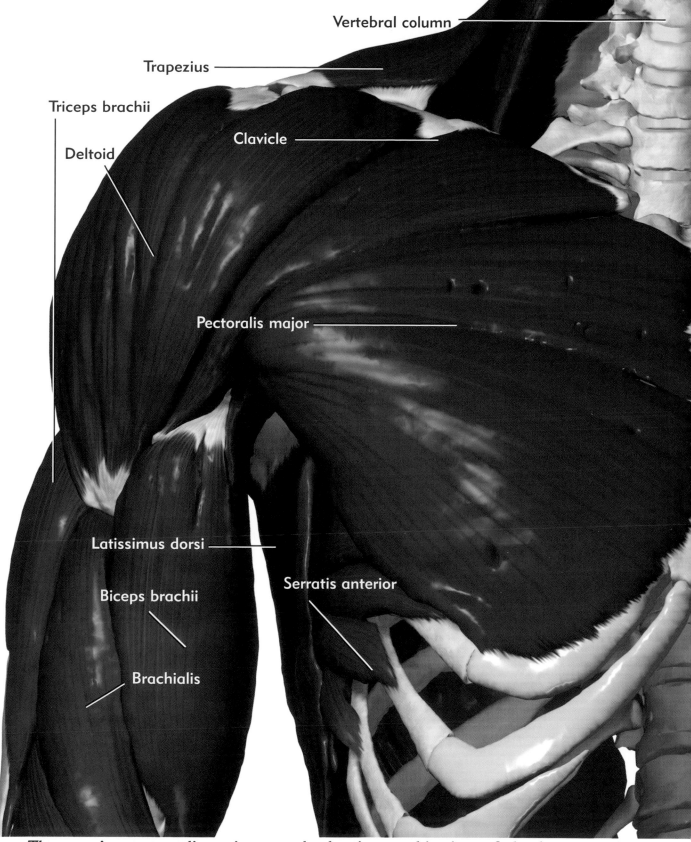

Vertebral column

Trapezius

Triceps brachii

Deltoid

Clavicle

Pectoralis major

Latissimus dorsi

Biceps brachii

Serratis anterior

Brachialis

The massive pectoralis major muscle dominates this view of the bones and muscles of the shoulder. Nine muscles cross the shoulder joint and control the movement of the upper arm.

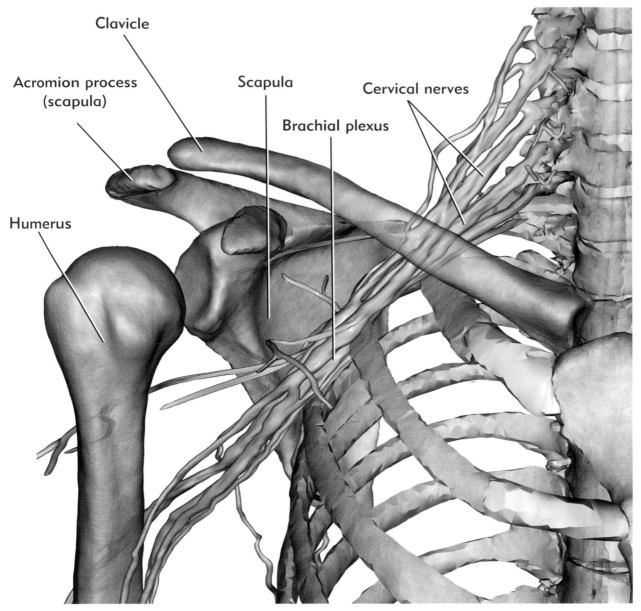

Clavicle

Acromion process
(scapula)

Scapula

Cervical nerves

Brachial plexus

Humerus

The ball joint where the humerus joins the shoulder is very flexible.

The purpose of most of the muscles and tendons of the shoulder is to let it move, whether up, down, or out. Other muscles help hold the shoulder girdle together. Ligaments keep muscles properly bound to bone; the word "ligaments" comes from a Latin word, *ligare*, meaning "to bind." Veins and arteries provide the shoulder and upper arm with oxygen-rich blood and remove oxygen-depleted blood, while nerves give the assemblage sensation.

One of the biggest upper body muscles is called the deltoid muscle, since it looks like the Greek letter delta. This powerful muscle starts on the clavicle and ends on the humerus. It helps hold the shoulder girdle together, but its main job is to raise the arm. Just above and behind the deltoid muscle is the trapezius muscle. This muscle is used in shrugging the shoulders up and down. Running from the clavicle down the front of the body is the pectoralis muscle, also known as the pectoral. This is the strong muscle used to push, shove, or lift things.

The triceps muscle starts on the scapula and runs down the back of the upper arm to the lower end of the humerus. This muscle allows the arm to move back. It also plays a role in moving the elbow, which is discussed in the next chapter.

The body's tendons, long, narrow, and stringlike, are like wires holding everything together, since they help the ligaments attach muscle to bone. And, like wires being pulled or released, tendons help the

Throwing a Ball

When a pitcher throws a baseball, most of his upper arm muscles come into play. First he prepares for the throw. He's using the deltoid muscles, which let him lift his arm up and back; the external rotators, which let him rotate his arm out; the trapezius muscle, which lets him raise his shoulder; and the rhomboids, which let him bring his shoulder back.

Next comes the pitch. The pitcher's internal rotators let him rotate his arm inward, and his triceps muscle gives him some of his throwing power (the rest comes from his legs and back). After the pitch, his trapezius and rotator muscles slow down, protecting his arm.

shoulder and upper arm to move. Two of the most important shoulder tendons are the rhomboid major and rhomboid minor. They both attach to the scapula and help the shoulder rotate out or in. Another major tendon is the levator scapulae, which does exactly what its name says. It helps raise and lower the scapula and the muscles around it.

Two major shoulder ligaments are the glenohumeral and the coracohumeral. They attach the ends of the humerus bone to the rest of the shoulder. Also in the shoulder are the bursae. Bursae contain synovial fluid, which acts like oil to keep everything in the shoulder from rubbing painfully together.

Arteries bring oxygenated blood into the shoulder, while veins circulate the blood back to the heart. The main arteries, which run like a river and its tributaries throughout the shoulder and arm, are the brachial and

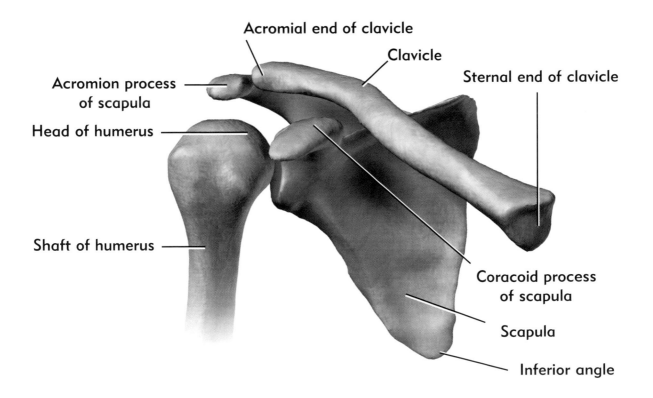

The bones of the shoulder form one of the most flexible joints in the human body, permitting movement in many directions.

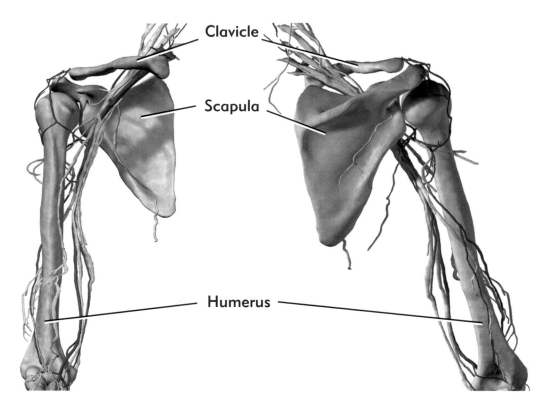

Clavicle

Scapula

Humerus

These anterior (front) and posterior (rear) views of the bones of the upper arm show the paths of supporting blood vessels and nerves.

axillary arteries. Veins also thread their way through; three of the major ones are called the cephalic, basilic, and median cubital.

The third network is made up of nerves. Without them, the body would have no sense of hot, cold, or pain. The network in the shoulder and upper arm includes the axillary nerve and the brachial nerve, plus their dozens of offshoots.

The most common injury to the shoulder is a fracture to one or more of the bones. A simple or clean fracture with no jagged edges is the easiest to heal, once a doctor has realigned the break and set it. The body's bone cells grow together to seal the break, and nerves, arteries, and veins weave themselves through. A complex fracture, one with more than one break or with broken bones poking through the skin, is more complicated to set and heal, particularly since there's also a chance of infection.

Sometimes a sports announcer will say that a baseball pitcher has damaged his rotary cuff. The rotary cuff is a group of four muscles that run from the scapula to the humerus. Their main job is to keep the shoulder girdle stable. But when they are torn or strained, which can happen to a pitcher's muscles, the arm can no longer move freely. In milder cases, rest may heal the injury, but worse cases may need surgery.

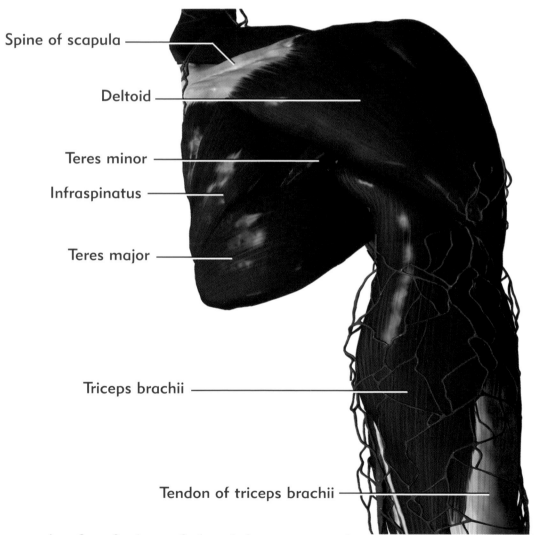

Spine of scapula

Deltoid

Teres minor

Infraspinatus

Teres major

Triceps brachii

Tendon of triceps brachii

This posterior (rear) view of the right arm reveals the bulging muscles that comprise the shoulder and upper arm. The triceps brachii is the powerful muscle that extends the forearm.

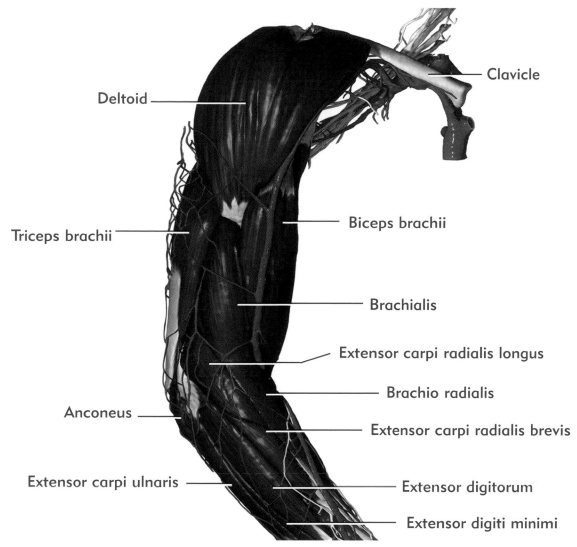

Clavicle

Deltoid

Triceps brachii

Biceps brachii

Brachialis

Extensor carpi radialis longus

Brachio radialis

Anconeus

Extensor carpi radialis brevis

Extensor carpi ulnaris

Extensor digitorum

Extensor digiti minimi

This is an anterior (front) view of the right arm. The biceps brachii flexes, or pulls in, the forearm. The extensor muscles of the forearm extend, or open, the fingers.

A fall or sharp blow can dislocate a shoulder, forcing the end of the humerus bone out of its socket. Movies show brave heroes popping their shoulders back into place and going on as though nothing has happened. In the real world, a doctor has to fit the humerus bone back into place, and the shoulder has to be rested for several weeks. A related injury is called shoulder separation, the stretching or tearing of the ligaments at the end of the clavicle so that it no longer meets the scapula. A separated shoulder also needs weeks of rest.

2
THE ARM
AND ELBOW

Since the humerus bone is rounded at the top, it would seem only logical for the lower end to be rounded, too. But instead of matching the rounded top that's part of the shoulder's ball-and-socket joint, the lower end of the humerus curves up and out to form a bowl. It becomes part of a different, but just as fascinating, type of joint: the hinge joint that forms the elbow.

The elbow is called a hinge joint because it opens and closes like the hinge on a door. It's designed to move the lower arm up or down, which is called flexion, or out and back, which is called extension. Though the elbow does let the lower arm move from side to side as well—which is called rotation—it doesn't move nearly as freely as the shoulder joint. The elbow needs that added stability since it has to be able to lift, lower, and hold objects, and do it accurately and securely.

The bowl-like end of the humerus bone forms the stable part of the hinge. Into it fit the two bones of the lower arm, the radius and the ulna, which form the moving part of the hinge. It's easy to see—and feel—this hinged motion in action. If the upper arm is held so that it doesn't move, the lower arm can still be raised and lowered thanks to the elbow joint. And if you keep one hand on your elbow while moving your arm, you can feel the hinge open and shut.

Because the elbow is less flexible than the shoulder, it has to be able to bear more stress. This wouldn't be possible without a network of strong ligaments to hold the three bones of the hinge joint together and let them move back and forth.

These ligaments are divided into two types according to where they attach to the elbow's bones. The first type is known as the lateral ligament complex. These are three allied ligaments located on the outer side—the lateral side—of the elbow. The three are called the ulnar collateral ligament, the radial collateral ligament, and the annular ligament. These names come from the bones to which the first two attach, the ulna and the radius, and the shape of the third one. The annular ligament, which caps the radius, is round. The first two work to support the humerus and ulna connection, while the third holds the radius in place.

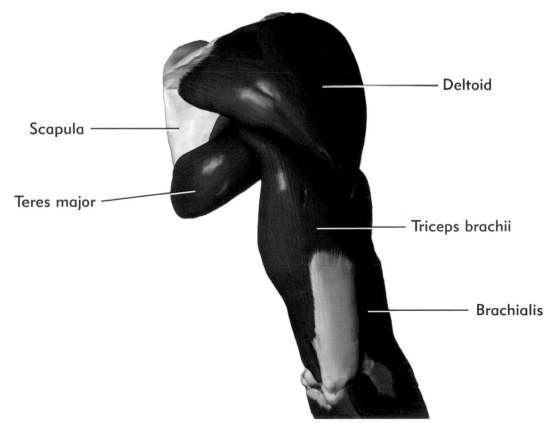

The powerful deltoid muscle extends, or lifts, the arm away from the body.

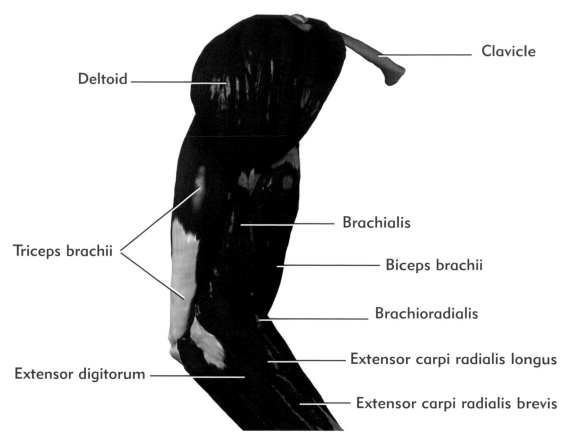

Deltoid

Clavicle

Brachialis

Triceps brachii

Biceps brachii

Brachioradialis

Extensor carpi radialis longus

Extensor digitorum

Extensor carpi radialis brevis

Because it bulges noticeably when the forearm is flexed, the biceps brachii is the muscle bodybuilders like to show off.

On the inner side of the elbow, known as the medial side, is the medial collateral ligament complex. Like the lateral ligament complex, it is made up of three related ligaments. These are the anterior band, the posterior band, and the transverse ligament. These names come from the ligaments' positions: front, back, and across the inner side of the elbow. These ligaments add more security to the elbow joint.

The elbow also has an added protection, called a joint capsule. This is a small envelope that fills in the space between the bone ends, and it both shields the bones and adds a smooth membrane, the synovial membrane. The synovial membrane is like a layer of oil that protects machine parts. It keeps them from rubbing together.

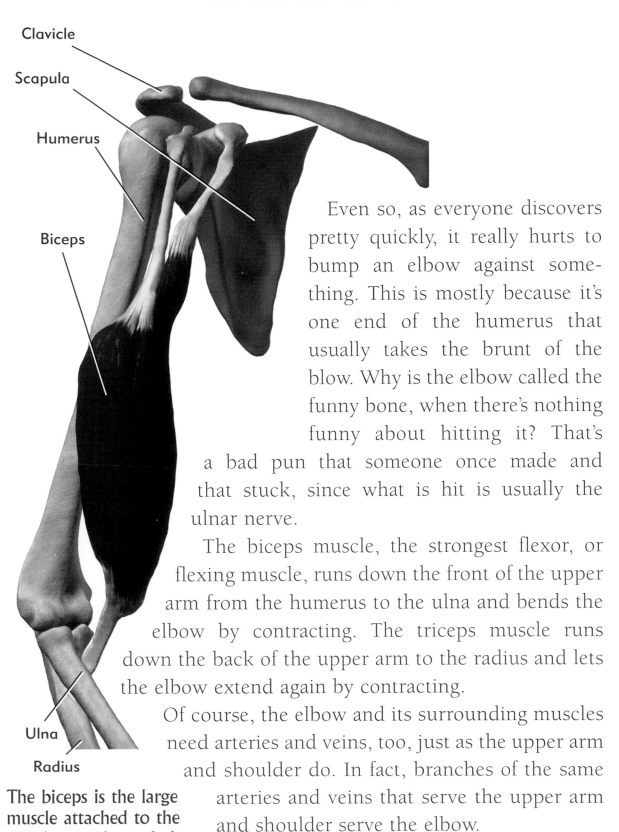

Clavicle

Scapula

Humerus

Biceps

Ulna

Radius

The biceps is the large muscle attached to the arm bones pictured above.

Even so, as everyone discovers pretty quickly, it really hurts to bump an elbow against something. This is mostly because it's one end of the humerus that usually takes the brunt of the blow. Why is the elbow called the funny bone, when there's nothing funny about hitting it? That's a bad pun that someone once made and that stuck, since what is hit is usually the ulnar nerve.

The biceps muscle, the strongest flexor, or flexing muscle, runs down the front of the upper arm from the humerus to the ulna and bends the elbow by contracting. The triceps muscle runs down the back of the upper arm to the radius and lets the elbow extend again by contracting.

Of course, the elbow and its surrounding muscles need arteries and veins, too, just as the upper arm and shoulder do. In fact, branches of the same arteries and veins that serve the upper arm and shoulder serve the elbow.

The elbow has its nerves, too, as anyone who has ever hit one of the nerves and felt their elbow tingle painfully knows. There are three main nerves: the median nerve, which runs down the arm through the biceps muscle; the radial nerve, which runs down the arm to the radius; and the ulnar nerve, which is the most easily injured of the three. It's the one most often bumped, in fact.

Since it is so easily bumped, the elbow can be seriously hurt as well. It's rare for there to be an actual break of the end of the humerus bone, but other problems can occur. The most dangerous injury is an elbow dislocation, since so many vital blood vessels and nerves run through the joint. Only a doctor should treat this type of injury.

The most familiar elbow injury, though far less serious than a dislocated elbow, is tennis elbow, so-called because it most often happens to tennis players. Tennis elbow is actually a form of tendonitis caused

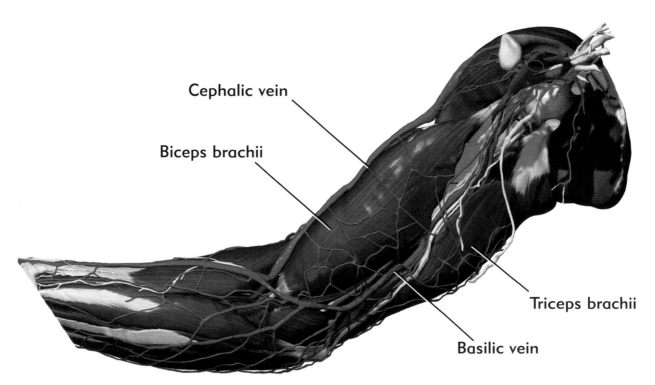

Cephalic vein

Biceps brachii

Triceps brachii

Basilic vein

The biceps and triceps muscles are clearly visible in this image of the upper arm. The major blood vessels and nerves are also shown.

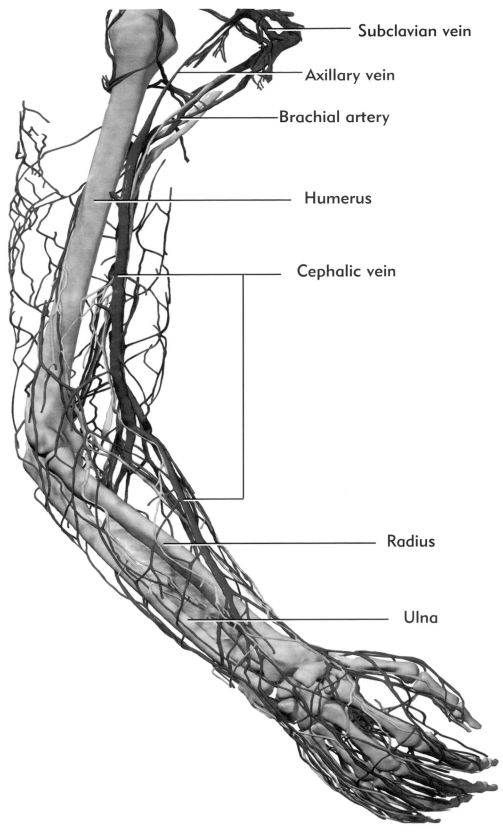

Subclavian vein

Axillary vein

Brachial artery

Humerus

Cephalic vein

Radius

Ulna

This view shows the bones, arteries, and veins of the right arm. The forearm and hand are together the most versatile limb in the entire animal kingdom.

Artificial Joints

The elbow is so vital a joint that for years anyone who had lost an arm just above the elbow had to face life with a replacement that couldn't bend properly or allow his or her arm normal strength and stability. Even the most advanced artificial elbow couldn't match the original for flexibility and stability.

But at NASA's Marshall Space Flight Center, scientists work on artificial joints for spacecraft, such as the improved arm of the space shuttle. They realized that the same technology could create a better elbow joint for humans. If the elbow joint they're designing works as well as the scientists expect, anyone receiving it will regain normal strength and stability. He or she will have benefited from the space age.

Humerus

Ulna

Radius

by irritating the elbow tendons through too much repetitive motion, such as serves and returns. Baseball pitchers can suffer from the same injury; it's called pitcher's elbow. And golfers call it golfer's elbow. In all cases, regardless of the cause, the treatment is the same: rest and anti-inflammatory medication.

It's also possible to hyperextend, or overextend, the elbow. That means bending it back beyond the safety point, like the hinge of a door being forced open too far. This is the sort of painful injury that can happen in a fall or a contact sport like football. Healing an overextended elbow involves a doctor's care and at least a week of rest.

The major bones of the arm

3
THE FOREARM AND HAND

O nly the upper ends of the ulna and radius bones go into the elbow joint. The two bones run down from the elbow to form the lower arm and end in the wrist. The ulna and radius are both slender, slightly curved bones ending where they join up with the bones that form the wrist. The ulna remains narrow along its entire length, widening only slightly at that point to meet about a third of the overall wrist, but the radius flattens out at the end to join with most of the wrist.

What's unusual about this two-boned forearm is that there's so much flex in it. It can be easily twisted right or left, with the radius and ulna neatly turning over each other. In fact, the turning of the two bones can actually be felt if you put a hand on your forearm and twist your forearm left and right. This easy turning is possible because the forearm has several smaller muscles, more than can be found in the upper arm.

For convenience, scientists break down the forearm muscles into two groups. The first group is called volar, which comes from the Latin for "palm" and means the underside—the palm side—of the arm. The second group is called dorsal, which means the top (or back) of the arm. The volar muscles and dorsal muscles are also broken up into two types. First, there is the superficial group. This name doesn't mean that the superficial muscles are not as important, merely that they're closer to the surface. Second, there's the deep group of muscles, which are literally deeper in the arm.

Looking at the names of the volar superficial group of muscles, it's pretty easy to figure out what muscles attach where and what they do. Flexor muscles do the flexing, and "radialis" refers to the radius bone. So the flexor carpi radialis is a flexing muscle that starts at the radius and runs down to the hand. The flexor carpi ulnaris starts at the ulna

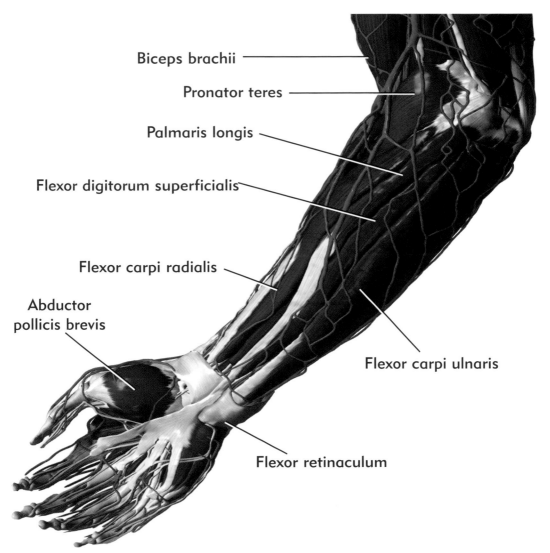

Biceps brachii

Pronator teres

Palmaris longis

Flexor digitorum superficialis

Flexor carpi radialis

Abductor pollicis brevis

Flexor carpi ulnaris

Flexor retinaculum

The muscles of the forearm control the movements of the hand, both flexing and extending the fingers and rotating the hand.

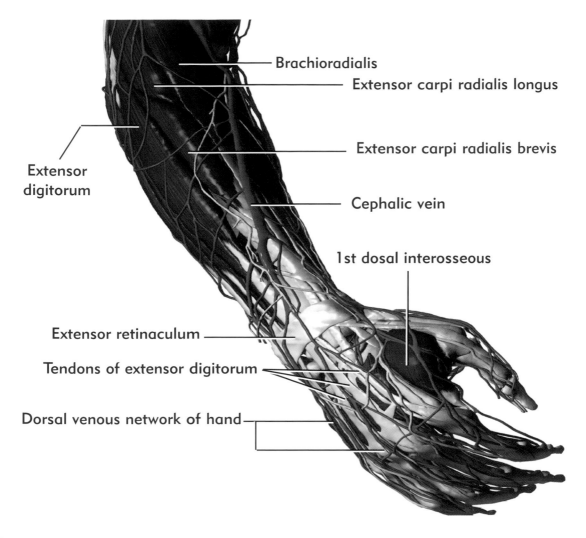

Brachioradialis

Extensor carpi radialis longus

Extensor carpi radialis brevis

Extensor digitorum

Cephalic vein

1st dosal interosseous

Extensor retinaculum

Tendons of extensor digitorum

Dorsal venous network of hand

The muscles of the forearm taper into long tendons that attach to the wrist, palm, or fingers.

and runs down to the hand as well. The word "digit" comes from the Latin word for "finger," so it's not too difficult, once you know that, to figure out that the flexor digitorum superficialis attaches to the fingers and lets them flex.

The muscle that lets the hand turn over doesn't have so easy a name to decode. It's called the pronator teres, from the Latin word *pronate*, which means "to turn over." The deep group of the volar muscles includes the flexor digitorum profundus, which also works on flexing the fingers, and the pronator quadratus, which works to turn the forearm over.

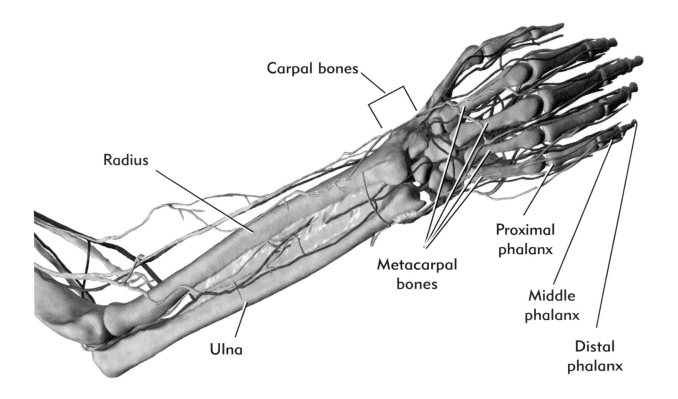

The brachioradialis muscle seen in isolation shows how the muscles of the forearm control the hand and the fingers.

The job of the dorsal muscles, the ones on the top (or back) of the arm, can mostly be puzzled out from their Latin names as well. We'll take the superficial group first. Logically, the opposite type of muscle to those that flex a limb would be those that extend it. The Latin word "extensor" is close enough to the English word "extend" to be understandable. So the extensor carpi radialis brevis—*brevis* means "brief"—is the short muscle that runs down from the radius and helps the forearm extend out. The extensor carpi radialis longus is the longer version that also helps the forearm extend, and the extensor carpi ulnaris is the version of an extension muscle that runs down from the ulna. The extensor digitorum extends the fingers.

24

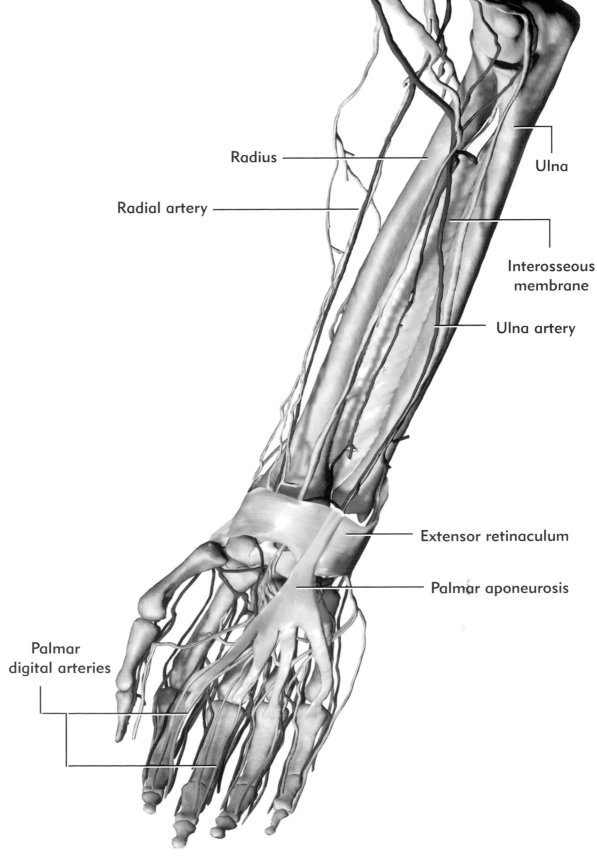

Radius

Ulna

Radial artery

Interosseous
membrane

Ulna artery

Extensor retinaculum

Palmar aponeurosis

Palmar
digital arteries

There are twenty-nine bones in the forearm: the radius, the ulna, and
twenty-seven bones in the hand and wrist.

Cephalic
vein

Radial
artery

The deep group of the dorsal forearm muscles includes one flexor muscle, the flexor digitorum profundis, which helps flex the fingers. The rest of this group are extensor muscles, including the extensor indicis and the extensor pollicis brevis and longus, all of which help extend the fingers. The last of the dorsal deep group of muscles is the abductor pollicis longus, which really is long, running down the entire forearm and ending in the fleshy base of the thumb.

So complex a system of muscles needs an equally complex system of arteries and veins, and of course has them. The forearm is fed by four branches of the ulnar artery and three from the radial artery. All four branches in turn have smaller branches throughout the forearm. In addition, the forearm has three interosseous arteries. "Osseous" means bony. Interosseous arteries run through spaces in the bones.

An equally complex network of veins takes the oxygen-poor blood from the forearm back for refreshing. Many of these forearm veins are branches of the major veins that run up into the upper arm and shoulder, such as the cephalic, basilic, and median cubital. These smaller branches

The radial artery supplies blood to the lateral muscles of the forearm.

are spread out through the forearm and hand like the many tributaries feeding into larger rivers.

The same concept is true of the network of nerves running through the forearm. The main nerves are the same ones that run through the elbow joint: the median, the radial, and the ulnar nerves. Off these three run the smaller web of nerves that give sensation to the entire forearm.

Injuries can happen to the forearm. It's very likely to get hurt in a fall or strained during a sports event. Most strains will heal with rest. But a break in the ulna or radius is more serious—as well as being the most common serious injury to happen to a forearm. The same treatments that are used on fractures of the humerus bone of the upper arm are used here, from setting to splinting, although a double break, like a compound fracture, is more difficult to set properly. Less common injuries, though still possible and quite

Protecting the Forearm

Rodeo riders often get hurt. The most likely to injure forearm muscles are bronc and bull riders, since a rider has to hang onto a rope attached to the bronc's halter or to the cinch around the bull's body—with only one hand. The whole strain of the ride goes through that arm. To prevent serious forearm injury, many riders bind up their forearms with what they call arm splints. These are overlapping wrappings of adhesive tape, angled up in a herringbone pattern and pulled tightly over the sorest part of the arm. They're left looser over the rest so that circulation isn't cut off.

painful, are displacements of the radius or ulna. These definitely need a doctor's care and possibly even surgery.

Less dramatic injuries come about through everyday wear and tear. Forearm muscles can be strained or even torn from lifting something heavy. Beginning weight lifters sometimes strain forearm muscles, but an awkward fall can stress the forearm as well. In both cases, the primary cure involves anti-inflammatory medicine and rest.

4
THE HAND

The forearm ends in what is certainly one of the most remarkable complexes of the human body: the wrist and hand. What makes the human hand so remarkable is its utter flexibility, its ability to move in almost any direction, and its ability to use and manipulate objects down to the literally smallest grain of rice. Every finger can move independently and flex at every joint. And what makes the complete flexibility even more amazing is that the hand is made up of many small bones and muscles, yet all of them work together perfectly. In fact, those many bones are exactly why the hand can move in so many ways. The hand also has what is called an opposable thumb, separate from the other fingers. It's the thumb that gives the hand the specific ability to pick up objects.

Eight small bones called carpals make up the wrist joint and join the hand to the radius and ulna in the forearm. The carpals include the scaphoid, lunate, triquetral, pisiform, hamate, capitate, trapezoid, and trapezium bones, most of them named in Latin for their basic shapes. The lunate bone, for instance, reminded scientists of the shape of the Moon, which the Romans called Luna. The word "carpal" simply means "wrist."

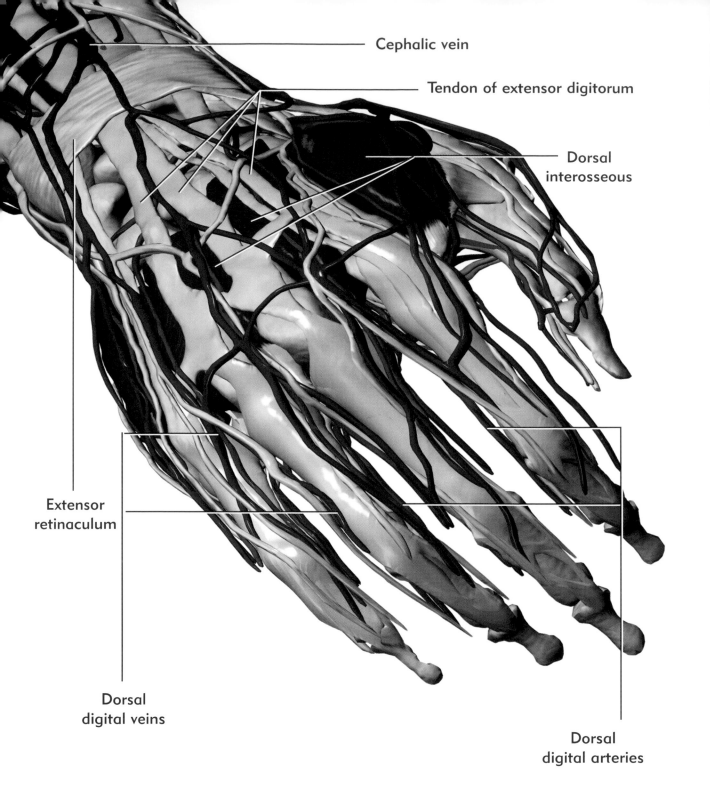

Cephalic vein

Tendon of extensor digitorum

Dorsal
interosseous

Extensor
retinaculum

Dorsal
digital veins

Dorsal
digital arteries

The muscles, nerves, and blood vessels of the hand. The hand can perform powerful and precise gripping movements, and it also has many sensory receptors, making it one of the most sensitive parts of the body.

Moving toward the hand from the carpals of the wrist, the next bones found are the metacarpals, the five long, thin bones that make up the hand. "Meta" means "bigger" or "greater." After that come the thinner phalanges, the bones of the fingers. Each finger is made up of three phalanges: the proximal—in closest proximity to the metacarpals—the middle, and the distal, or most distant. The distal phalanges are the smallest of the three and the ones that bear the human nails. It's these many bones that give the hand and wrist their amazing flexibility, as well as the way the thumb is set off from the rest of the fingers, that gives the hand its dexterity.

Many of the muscles of the hand have already been mentioned in the section on the forearm. But so complex a structure needs to have many smaller muscles as well to give it agility. The abductor pollicis brevis is a muscle of the thumb alone, as is the flexor pollicis brevis and the adductor pollicis, while the opponens pollicis is the muscle

Putting Spin on the Ball

A baseball pitcher would be unable to pitch without hand dexterity. To throw a fastball, a pitcher grips the baseball with his or her first two fingers about half an inch apart and perpendicular to the widest point of the ball's seam. The pitcher's thumb is on the underside of the ball, also perpendicular to the seam. He or she winds up, adding power to the pitch, then throws the ball from the tips of the fingers. If the pitcher wants to make the pitch a little slower but more difficult to hit, he or she gives a small snap of the wrist when releasing the ball to give it an added backward spin.

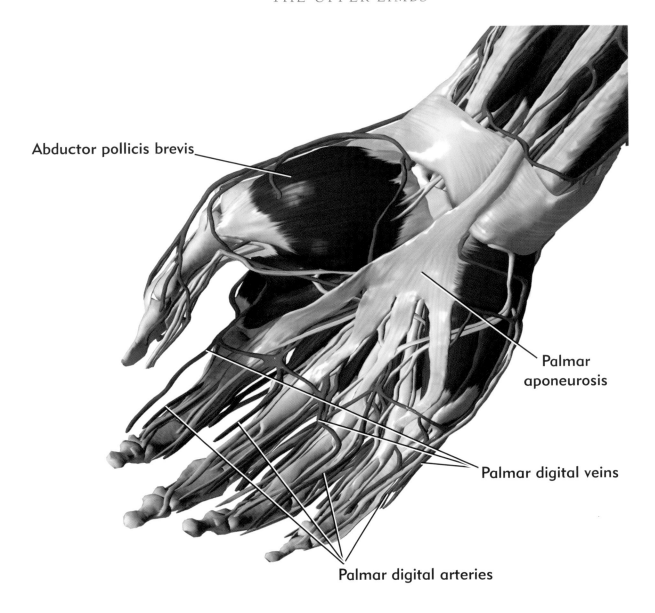

Abductor pollicis brevis

Palmar aponeurosis

Palmar digital veins

Palmar digital arteries

Digital arteries supply blood to the fingers. The abductor pollicis brevis muscle manipulates the thumb.

that lets the thumb "oppose" the fingers. The name of the palmaris brevis should show that it's a short muscle of the palm; it helps the hand grip. The fingers have their smaller muscles as well. The flexor digiti minimi brevis is the "small finger flexing muscle," and the opponens digiti minimi lets the thumb and the fifth finger, the pinky, touch each other. There are still more muscles for flexing and

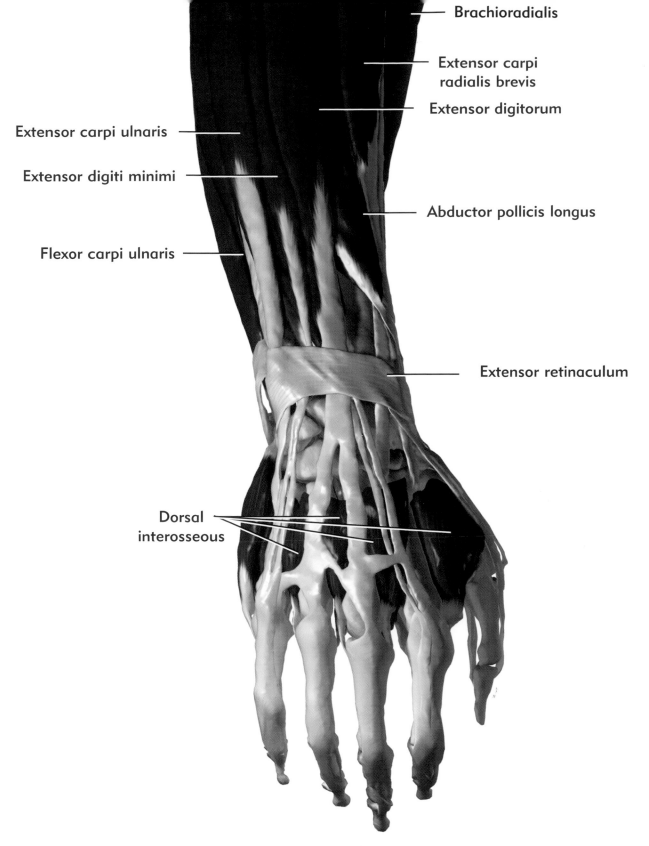

Brachioradialis

Extensor carpi radialis brevis

Extensor digitorum

Extensor carpi ulnaris

Extensor digiti minimi

Abductor pollicis longus

Flexor carpi ulnaris

Extensor retinaculum

Dorsal interosseous

The muscles and tendons of the right hand. The interosseous muscles are small muscles in the hand itself that assist the flexor and extensor muscles of the forearm in manipulating the fingers.

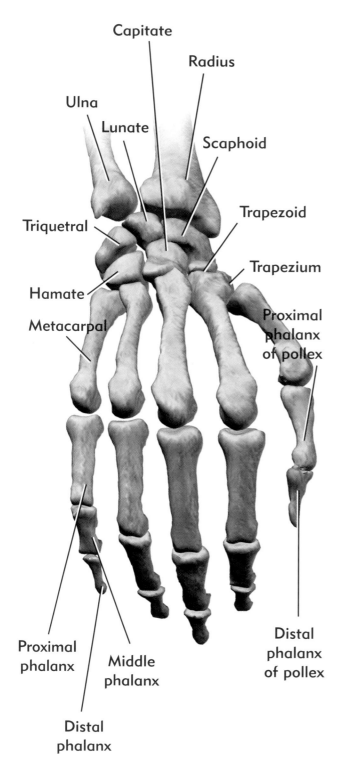

Capitate

Radius

Ulna

Lunate

Scaphoid

Triquetral

Trapezoid

Trapezium

Hamate

Metacarpal

Proximal phalanx of pollex

Proximal phalanx

Middle phalanx

Distal phalanx of pollex

Distal phalanx

extending the fingers: the dorsal interossei and the lumbricals. All in all, there are twenty-seven muscles in the hand.

The two main nerves of the hand are the median and ulnar, the ones that run down the arm and branch out into the fingers into a fine network that gives them great sensitivity.

The hand is constantly refreshed by oxygenated blood from a network of articular arteries, which branch down through the wrist from the ulnar and radial arteries. Depleted blood is taken away by a network of veins that are branches of the major arm veins: the cephalic, basilic, and median cubital. Part of this network can easily be seen as the blue lines on the back of the hand or the underside of the wrist.

Because the hand and wrist are so complex, they're also easy to injure. Almost everyone has experienced the pain of catching a finger in a door or of banging a fingertip so hard the nail is damaged.

The bones of the hand are divided into three groups: the carpal bones of the wrist, the metacarpal bones of the palm, and the phalanges of the fingers.

Those accidents are painful, but they heal relatively quickly and don't require a doctor's help unless there's a suspicion of fracture. True fractures usually involve one or more of the metacarpal bones of the fingers. Just as with fractures of the larger arm bones, a fracture of a finger must be set by a doctor and splinted.

One hand and wrist problem that has become increasingly common in our modern world is called carpal tunnel syndrome. This is an injury to the median nerve as it enters the wrist through a bony canal formed by the transverse carpal ligament. Carpal tunnel syndrome occurs when the nerve is compressed or pinched by the ligament. This compression is the start of a problem that can only grow progressively worse if nothing is done to correct it. Carpal tunnel syndrome leads to pain in the wrist, numbness or tingling in the hand, a "pins and needles" type of sensation in the hand at

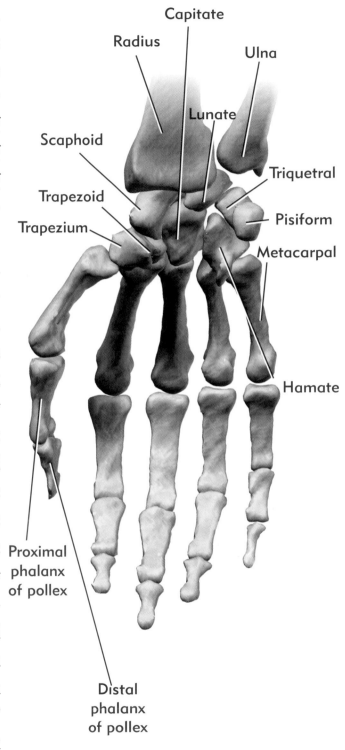

The large number of joints between the bones of the hand give the hand great flexibility.

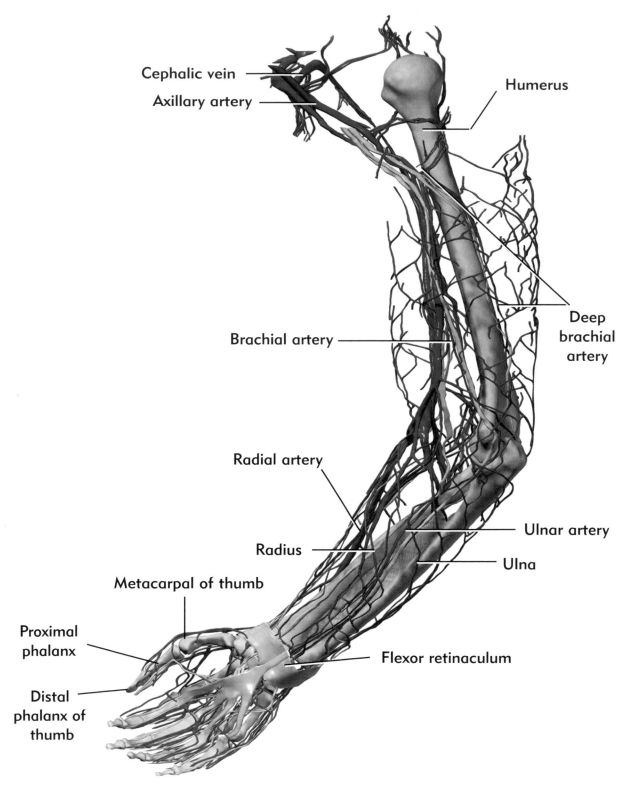

Cephalic vein

Axillary artery

Humerus

Brachial artery

Deep brachial artery

Radial artery

Ulnar artery

Radius

Ulna

Metacarpal of thumb

Proximal phalanx

Flexor retinaculum

Distal phalanx of thumb

This image of the right arm reveals the bones and blood vessels.

night, weakening of the hand, and possibly permanent damage. The cause of the pinching or compressing of the nerve is forceful but repetitive hand movements, such as those of a typist, an assembly line worker, or a checkout clerk in a supermarket.

For a long time, women were the primary sufferers of carpal tunnel syndrome, primarily because more women than men occupied the lower paying jobs that required repetitive motion. In fact, there have been several lawsuits on that issue. But it's an ironic fact that the computer age has resulted in both greater equality between women and men in the workplace and more male sufferers of carpal tunnel syndrome.

In its early stages, the problem can be removed by simply modifying work activities and using anti-inflammatory medicines. But if carpal tunnel syndrome isn't treated, it can lead to serious injury that may require surgery and may even end in permanent damage.

But most of us use our hands without ever suffering a major injury. Once we leave childhood, we take them for granted. Without the incredible flexibility and dexterity that our hands give us, whether we're working on something small or large, we would never be able to design or build anything, create any art, or play most sports. We would never have become truly human.

GLOSSARY

arteries   Narrow tubes that bring oxygen-rich blood to the limbs.

bursae   Protective pads of synovial fluid found in the shoulder girdle; bursa is the singular form of bursae.

carpal   One of the bones that make up the wrist.

carpal tunnel syndrome   Condition caused by the medial nerve being pinched by the transverse carpal ligament; caused by repetitive hand movements.

clavicle   A slender, curved bone at the front of the shoulder; also called the collarbone.

extensor   Muscle used to extend a limb.

fastball   Pitch in baseball that is faster than other types of pitches.

flexor   Muscle used for flexing a limb.

humerus Long bone of the upper arm.

metacarpal Bone of the hand in the section between the wrist and the fingers.

nerves Cells that transmit sensations between the brain and the body.

nervous system Wirelike network that goes throughout the body transmitting nerve impulses.

opposable Opposite in position from something else, as in "an opposable thumb is opposite the rest of the fingers."

phalanx Finger bone. There are three phalanges in each finger.

radius Shorter of the two forearm bones. The other is the ulna.

rotary cuff Four shoulder muscles that keep the shoulder stable.

scapula Wide, flatter bone at the back of the shoulder. It's also known as the shoulder blade.

synovial fluid Smooth substance that keeps the ends of bones from grinding against each other.

tendonitis Inflammation of the tendons due to overuse or repetitive motion.

tennis elbow Form of tendonitis common to tennis players; also called pitcher's elbow or golfer's elbow.

thorax Cavity or space inside the chest formed by the twelve thoracic vertebrae, the twelve pairs of ribs, and the sternum.

ulna The longer of the two forearm bones. The other is the radius.

veins The narrow network of tubes that take oxygen-depleted blood back to the heart for refreshing.

FOR MORE INFORMATION

Organizations

Department of Health and Human Services
200 Independence Avenue SW
Washington, DC 20201
(202) 619-0257
Web site: http://www.os.dhhs.gov

U.S. National Library of Medicine
8600 Rockville Pike
Bethesda, MD 20894
Web site: http://www.nlm.nih.gov

Web Sites

Anatomy-Resources.Com
http://www.anatomy-resources.com
This is a serious site with a humorous look. For those whose lives won't be complete without a plastic—or, for that matter, a real—skeleton or poster of anatomy. The home page, by the way, features a chorus line of dancing skeletons.

BodyQuest

http://Library.thinkquest.org/10348/home.html

The home page of BodyQuest features a search engine, indices, quizzes, and a body map.

The Electronic Textbook of Hand Surgery

http://www.eatonhand.com

This is the home page of e-Hand.com, which features anything medical to do with the hand. Subjects range from anatomy to therapy.

A Guided Tour of the Visible Human Project

http://www.madsci.org/~lynn/VH

This is a good overall guide to the project, which now has over 18,000 digitized sections of the body. The Visible Human Project is the source for the digital images in this book.

HealthWeb

http://www.healthweb.org

A mega-search site with links to anatomy as well as many other medical subjects.

A Patient's Guide to Common Shoulder Problems

http://www.medicalmultimediagroup.com/pated/
    shoulder_problems.html

This is a comprehensive site that includes advice on the care and treatment of all kinds of shoulder injuries. It's a good source of information on what can go wrong and how it can be cured.

The Southern California Orthopedic Institute

http://www.scoi.com

Although aimed primarily at medical professionals and their patients, this medical site features good illustrations of the human skeleton, as well as clear explanations about the various bones and muscles.

Sports Medicine

http://sportsmedicine.about.com/health/sportsmedicine/cs/baseball

This is a basic search engine page that features numerous links to information about common baseball injuries. A good place to start.

FOR FURTHER READING

Alexander, R. McNeill, and Brian Kosoff. *Bones: The Unity of Form and Function*. Boulder, CO: Westview Press, 2000.

Clayman, Charles. *Illustrated Guide to the Human Body*. New York: DK Publishing, 1995.

Garrick, James, and Peter Radetsky. *Anybody's Sports Medicine Book: The Complete Guide to Quick Recovery from Injuries*. Berkeley, CA: Ten Speed Press, 2000.

Germain, Blandine C. *Anatomy of Movement*. Seattle, WA: Eastland Press, 1993.

Kapit, Wynn. *The Anatomy Coloring Book*. Reading, MA: Addison-Wesley Publishing Company, 1993.

McCabe, Steven J., and Stan Goldman. *The Hand, Wrist, and Arm Sourcebook*. Los Angeles: Lowell House, 1999.

Netter, Frank H. *Atlas of Human Anatomy*. New York: Novartis Medical Education, 1997

Parker, Steve. *Eyewitness: Skeleton*. New York: DK Publishing, 2000.

Siegel, Irwin M. *All About Bone: An Owner's Manual*. New York: Demos Medical Publishing, 1998.

Waldby, Catherine. *The Visible Human Project: Informatic Bodies and Posthuman Medicine*. New York: Routledge, 2000.

INDEX

About the Author

Josepha Sherman is a professional author and folklorist, with more than 40 books and 125 short stories and articles in print. She is an active member of the Authors Guild and the Science Fiction Writers of America. Her Web site is at http://www.josephasherman.com.

Photo Credits

All digital images courtesy of Visible Productions, by arrangement with Anatographica, LLC.

Series Design

Claudia Carlson

Layout

Tahara Hasan